COLORING CUBES
Coloring Book

Benjamin Allen

All rights reserved. This book is protected by the copyright laws of the United States of America. This book may not be copied or reprinted for commercial gain or profit. No part of this publication may be reproduced, distributed, or transmitted in any form or by any means or stored in a database or retrieval system without prior written permission of the Publisher.

Copyright © 2016 Benjamin Allen

www.portraitsthatbreathe.com

All rights reserved.

ISBN-13: 978-1987713558

ISBN-10: 1987713559

Front and back cover artwork, by Benjamin Allen

DEDICATION

This book is dedicated to all who are young at heart.
You are never too young, or to old, to enjoy coloring

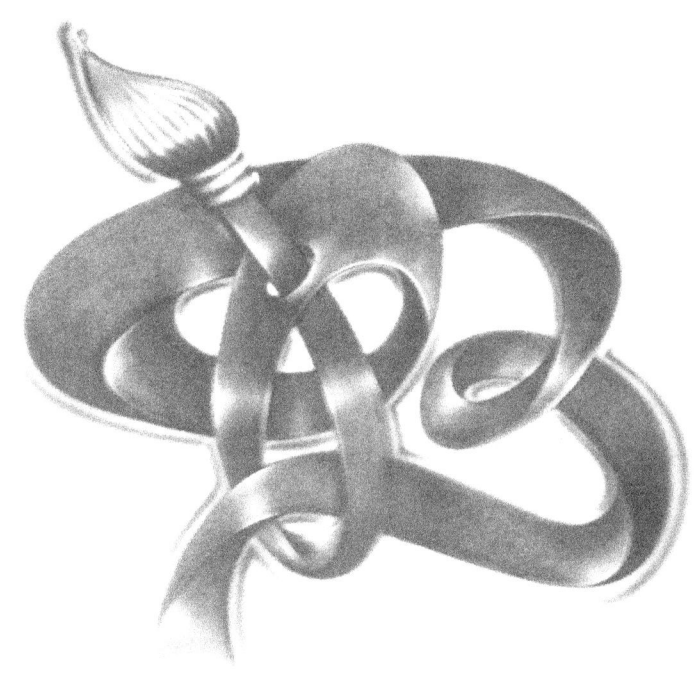

PORTRAITSTHATBREATHE

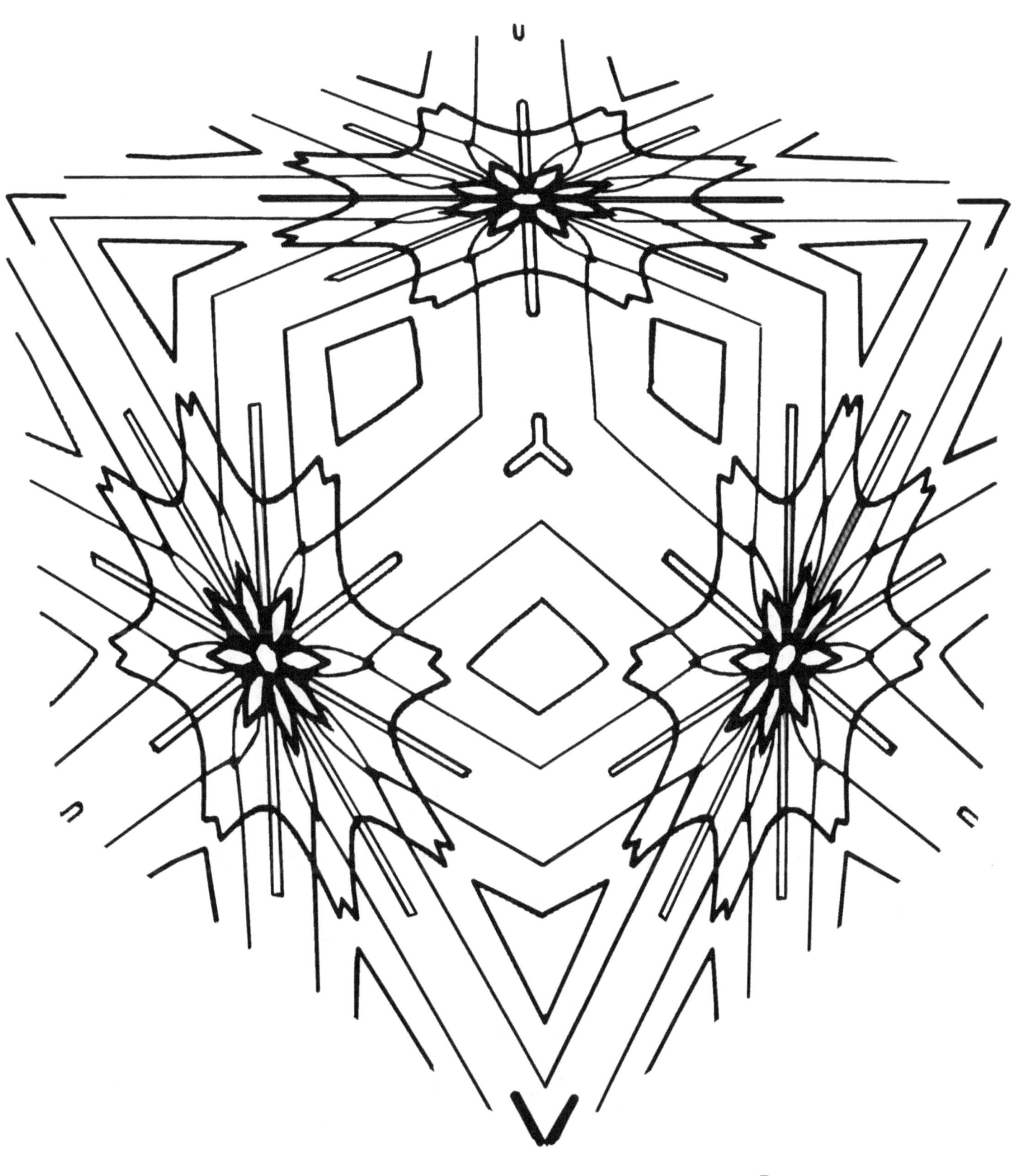

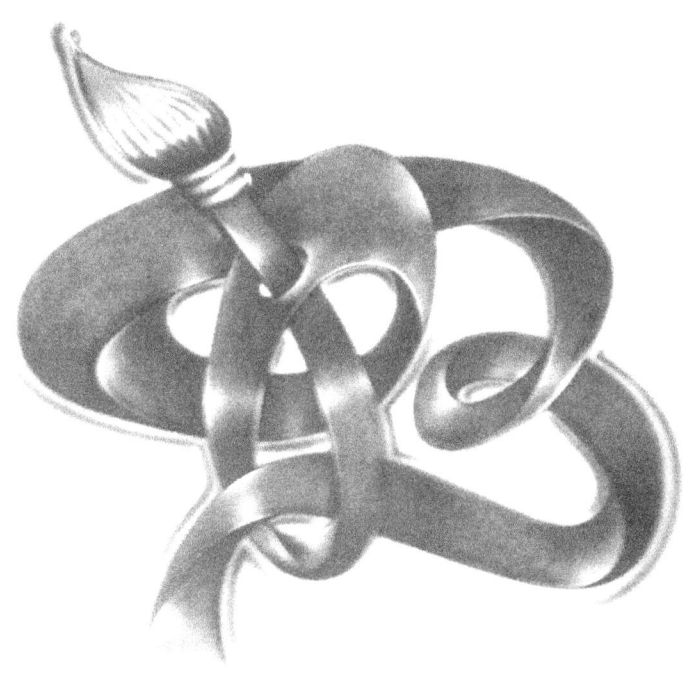

PORTRAITSTHATBREATHE

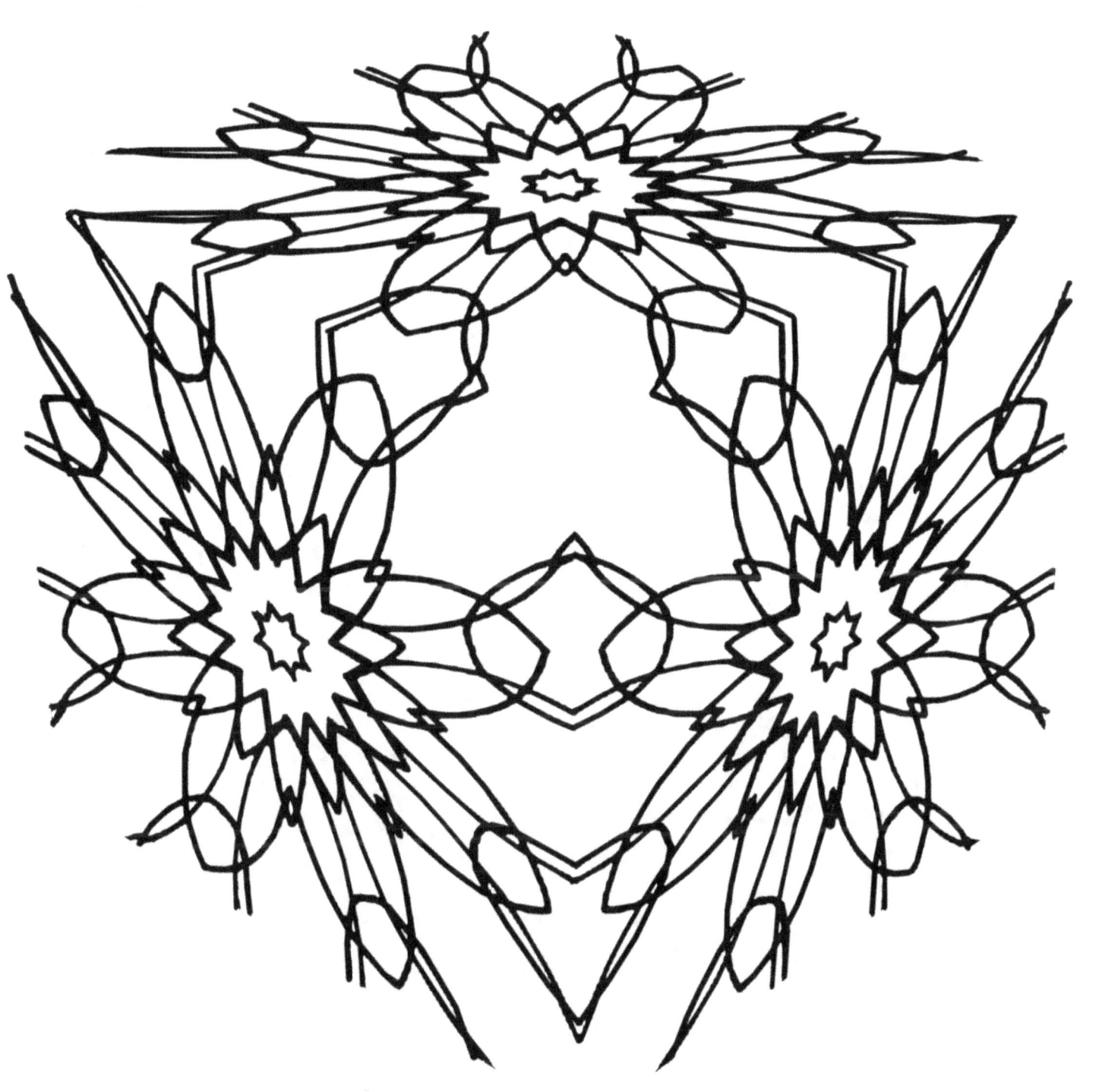

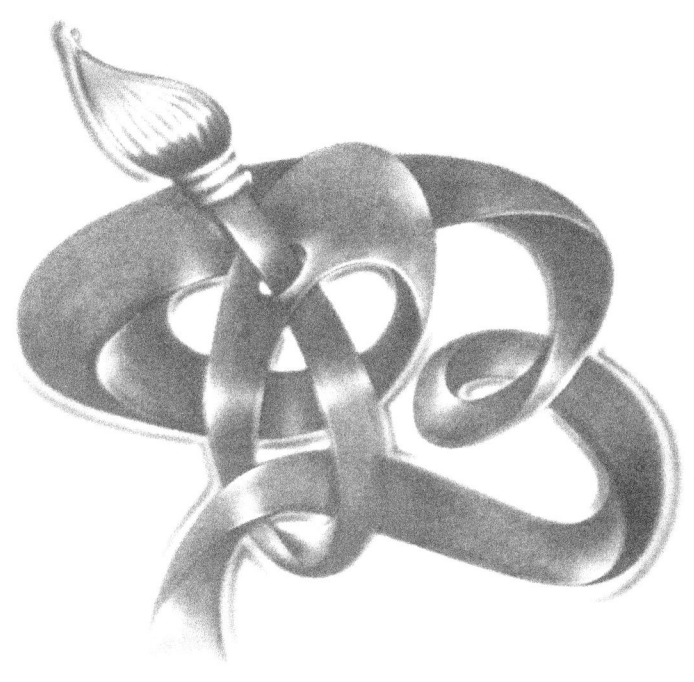

PORTRAITSTHATBREATHE

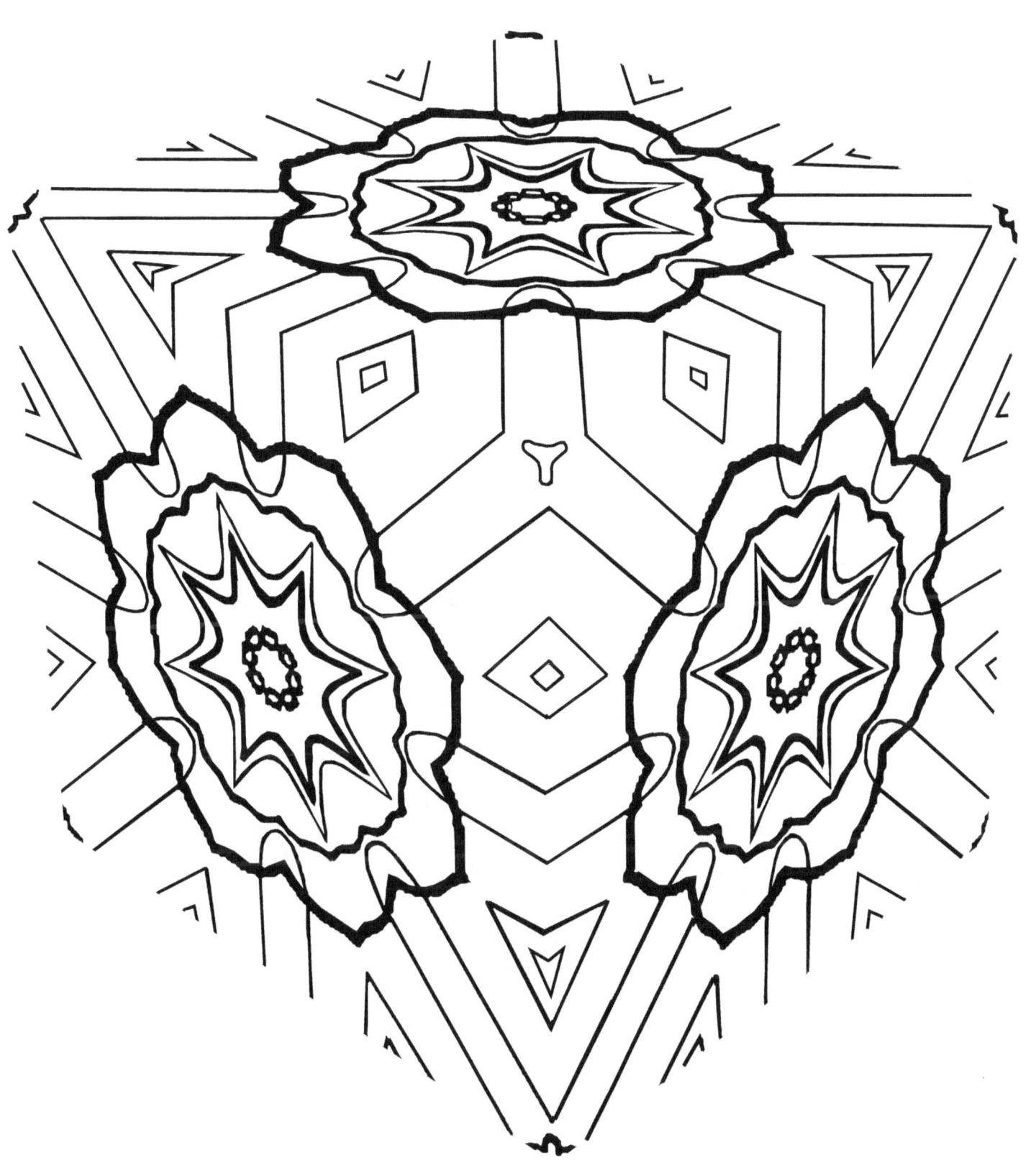

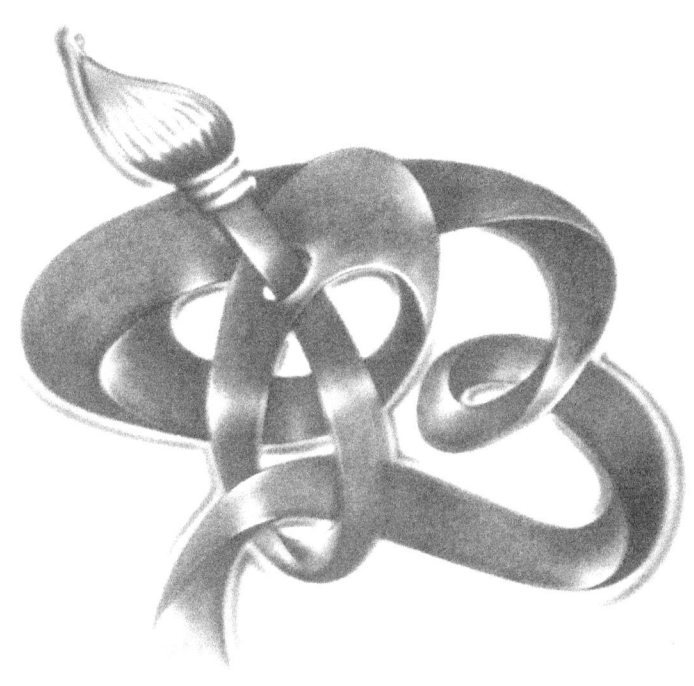

PORTRAITSTHATBREATHE

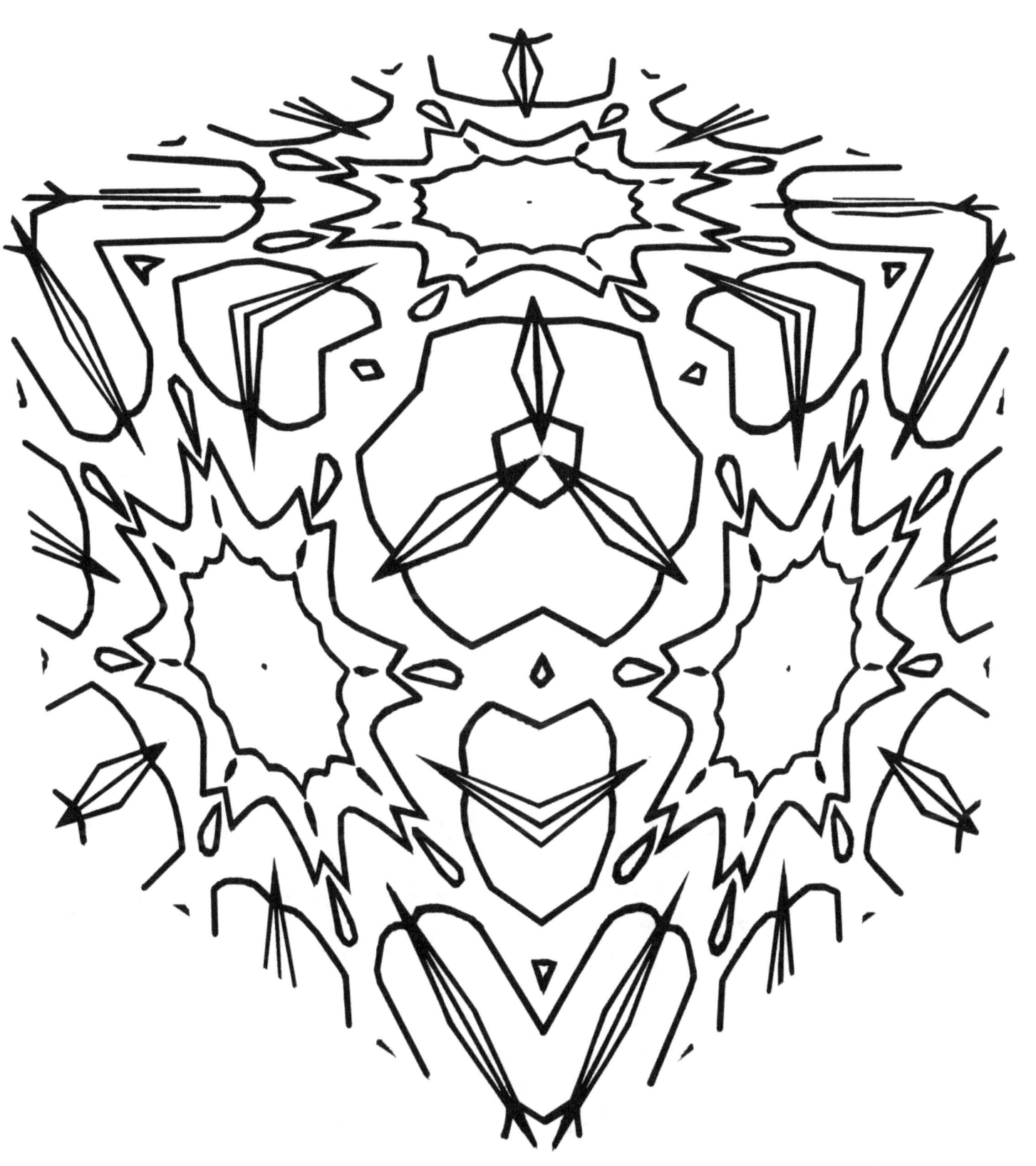

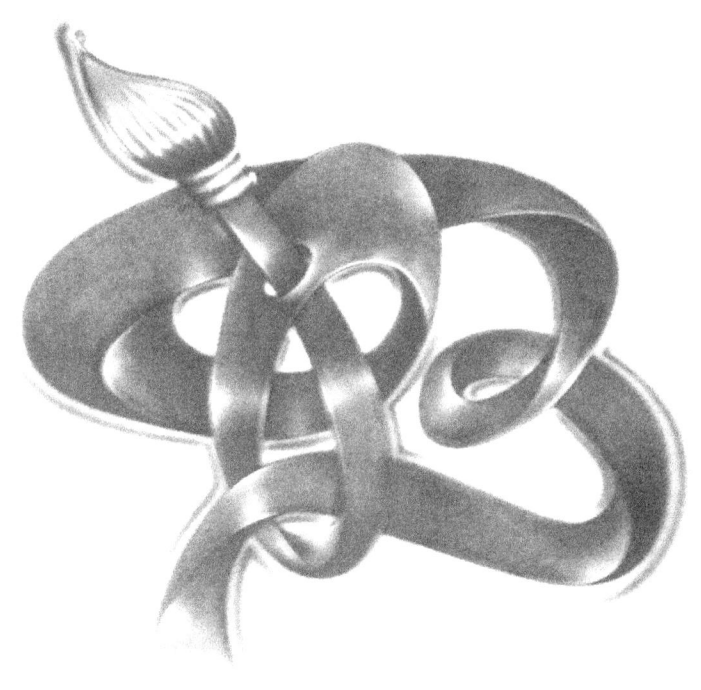

PORTRAITSTHATBREATHE

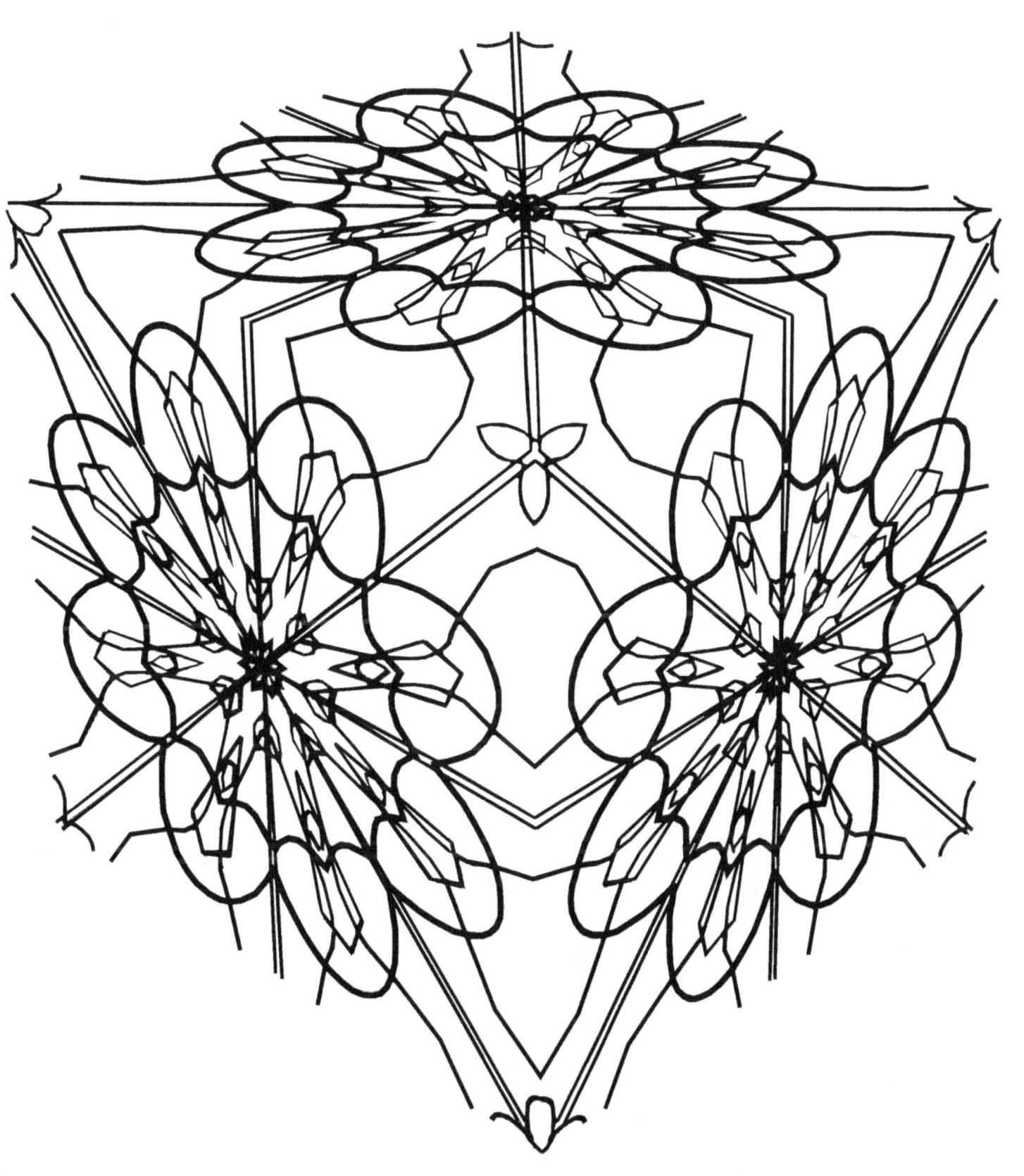

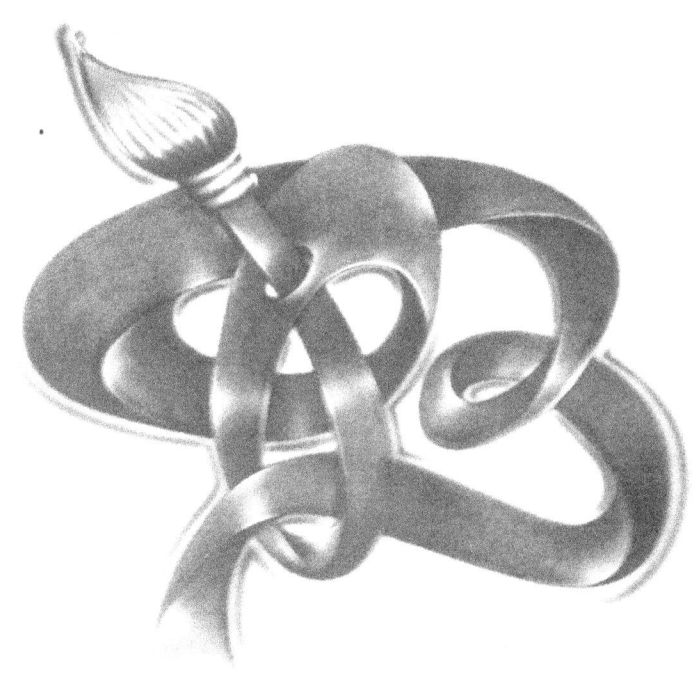

PORTRAITSTHATBREATHE

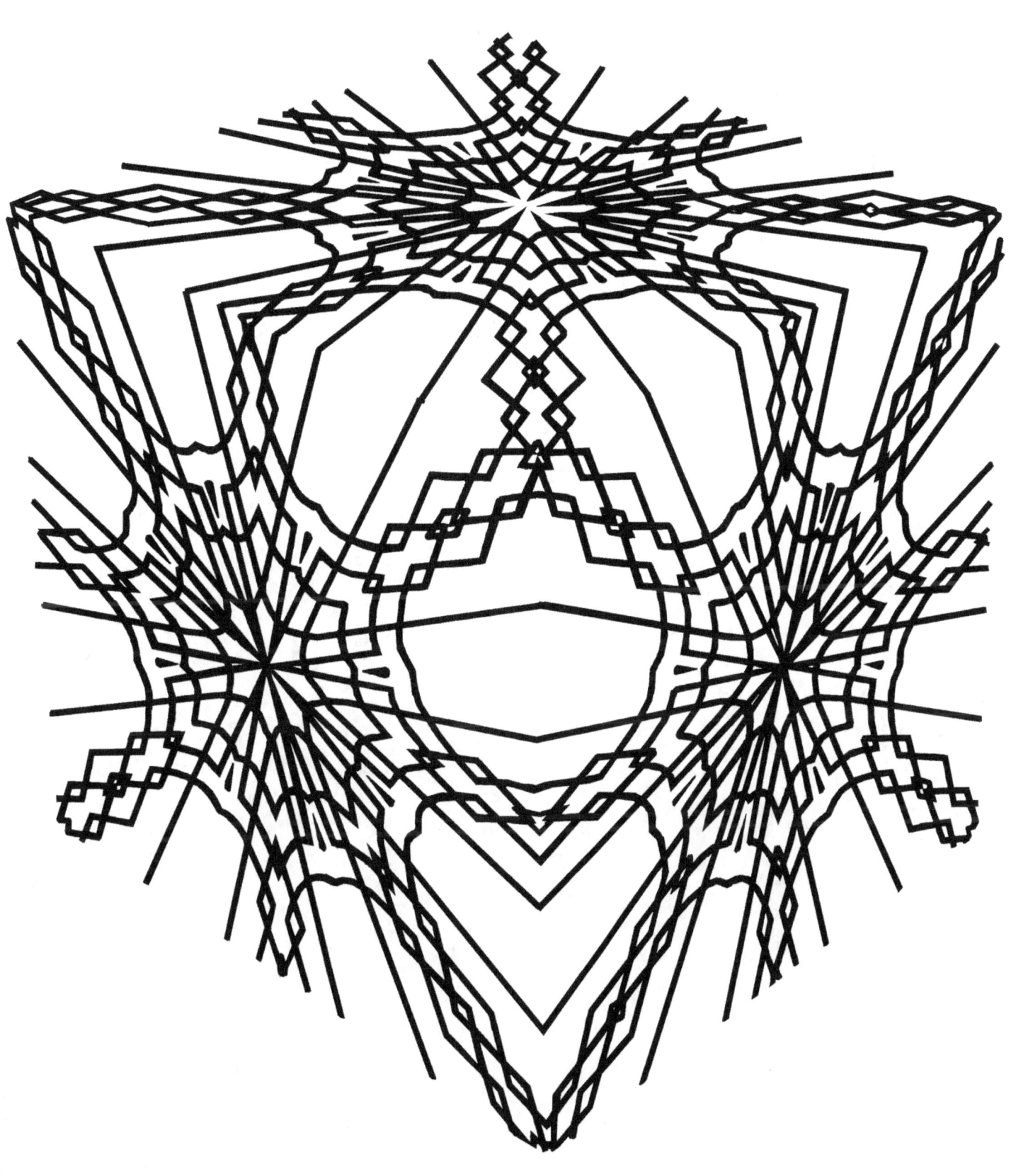

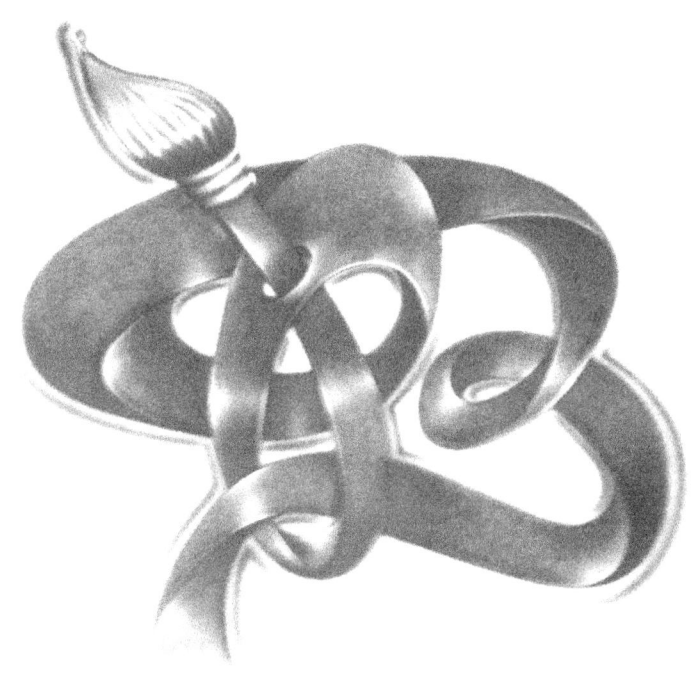

PORTRAITSTHATBREATHE

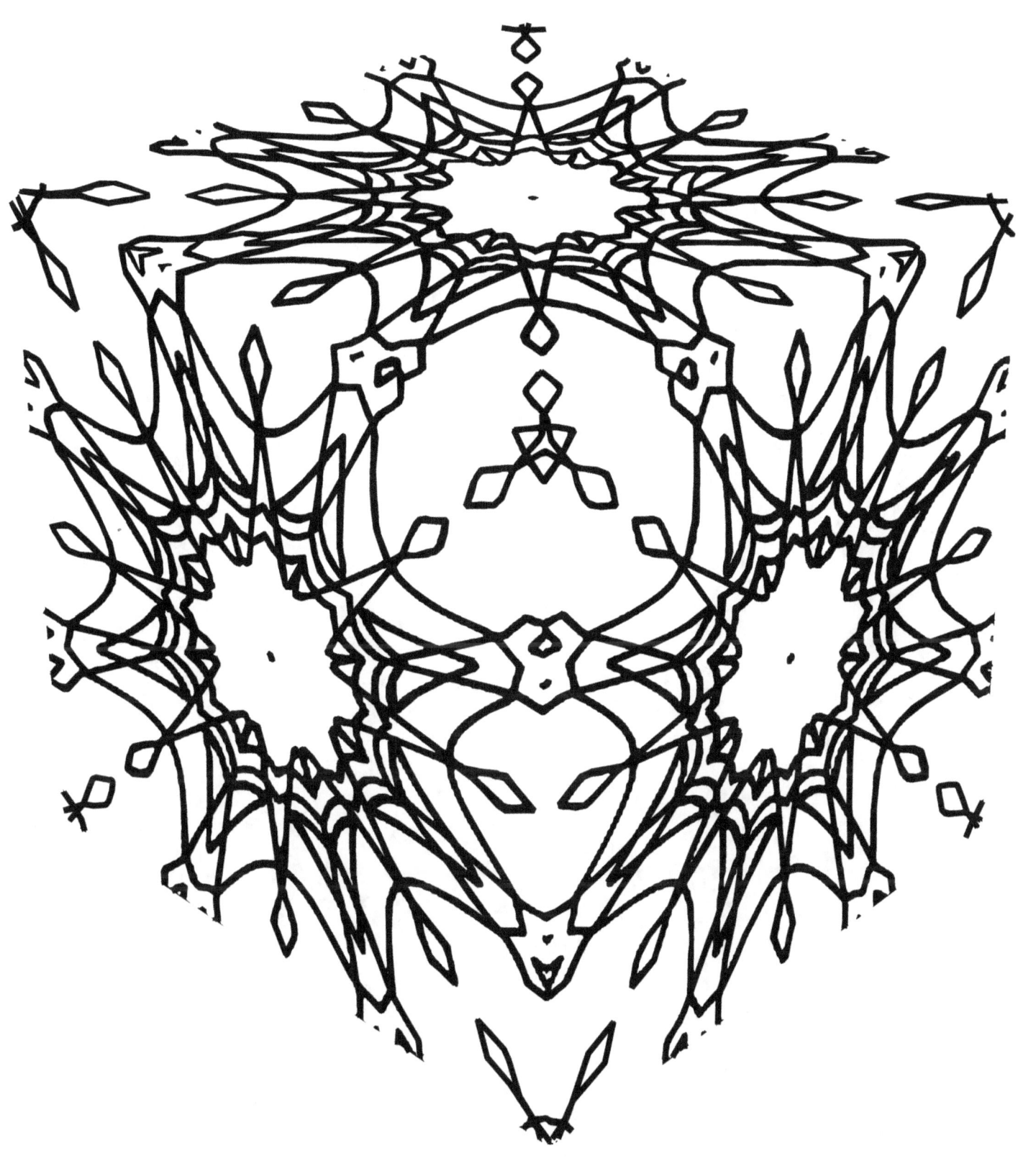

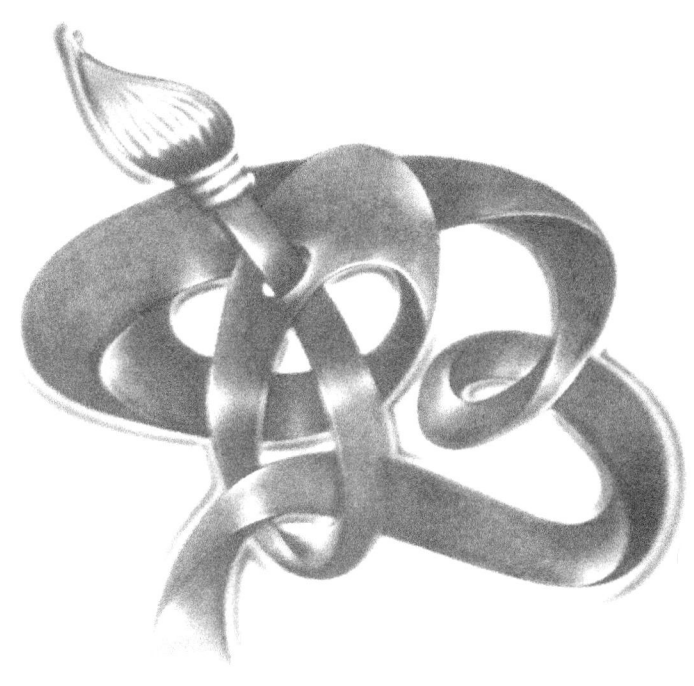

PORTRAITSTHATBREATHE

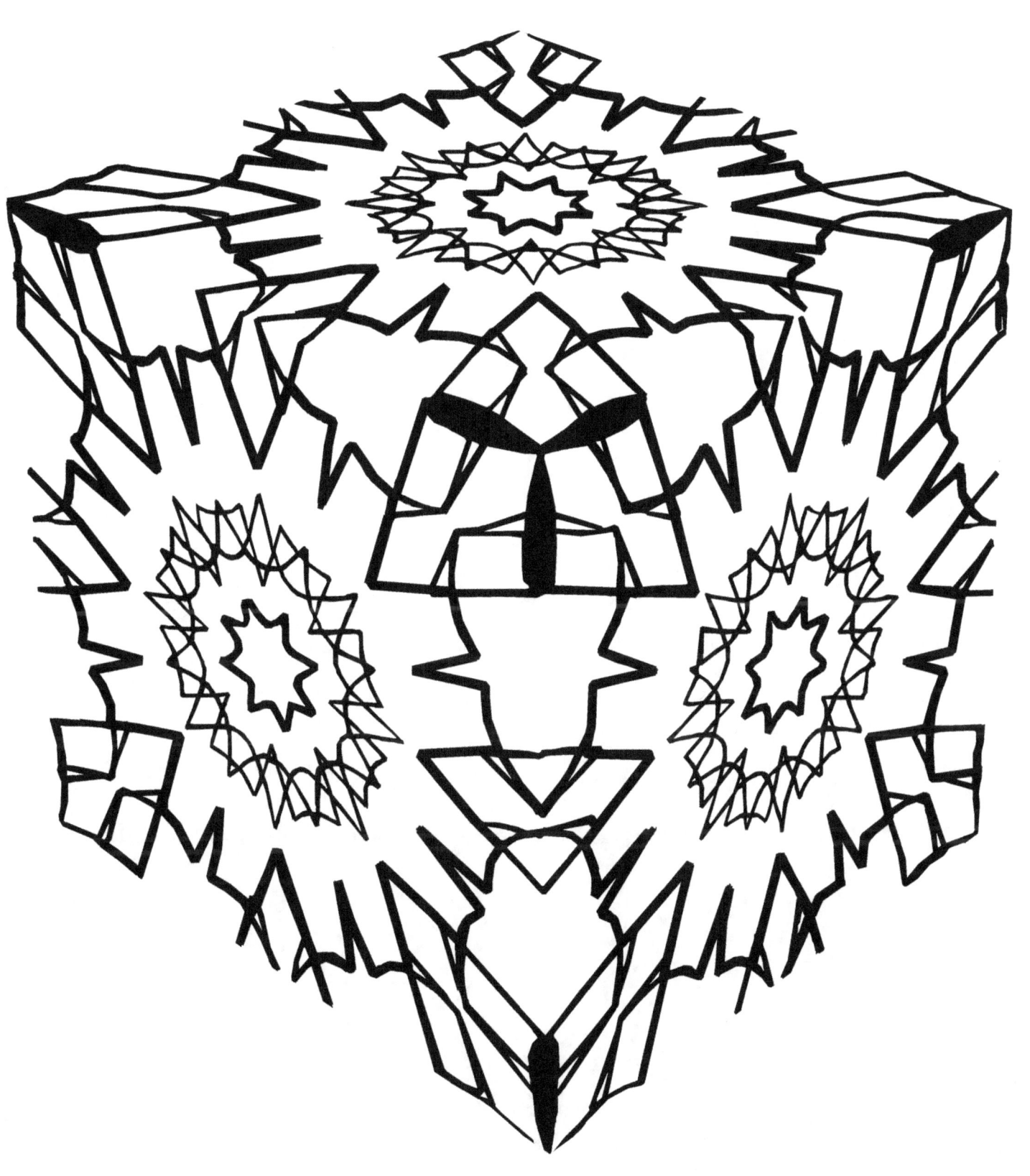

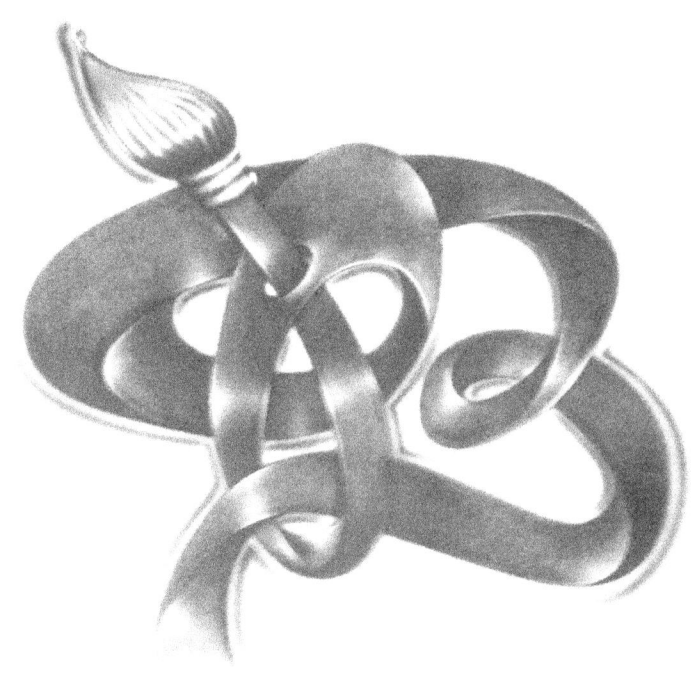

PORTRAITSTHATBREATHE

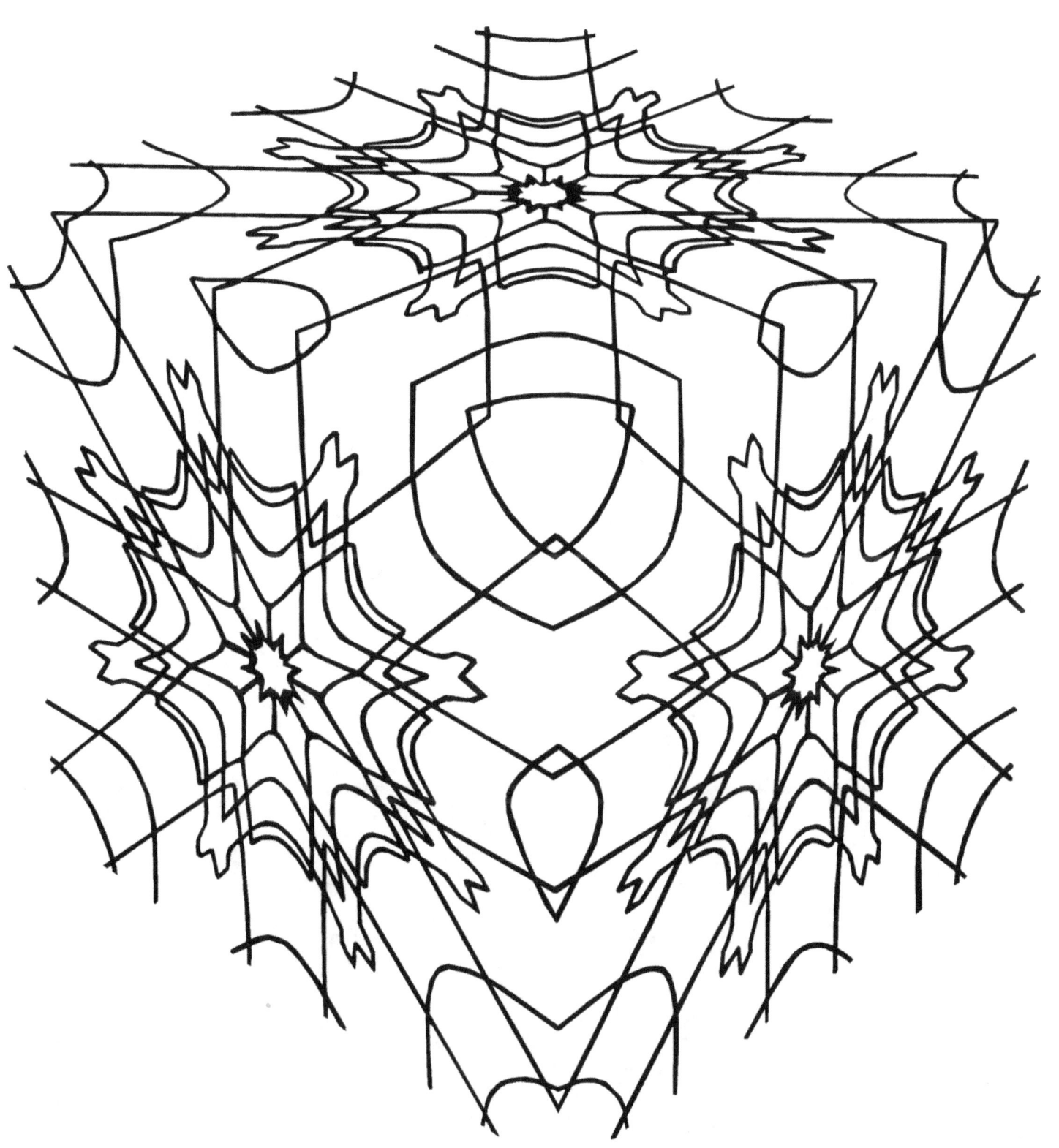

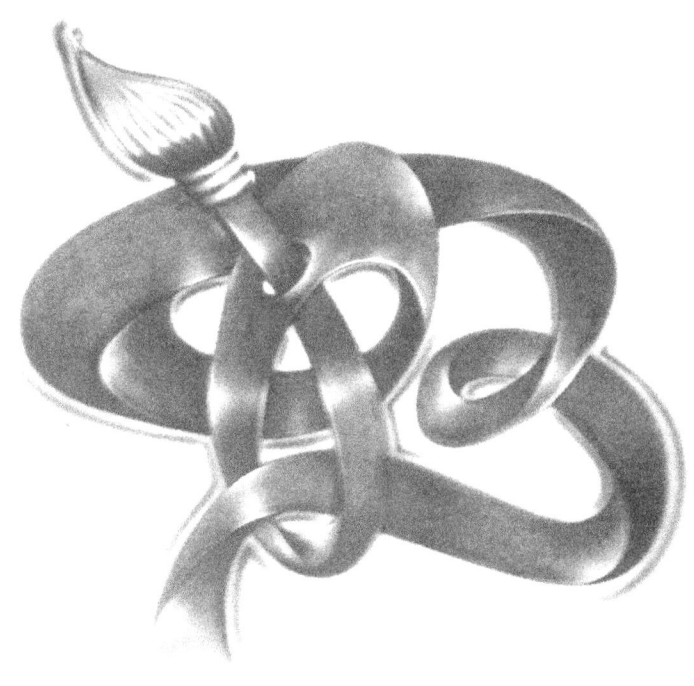

PORTRAITSTHATBREATHE

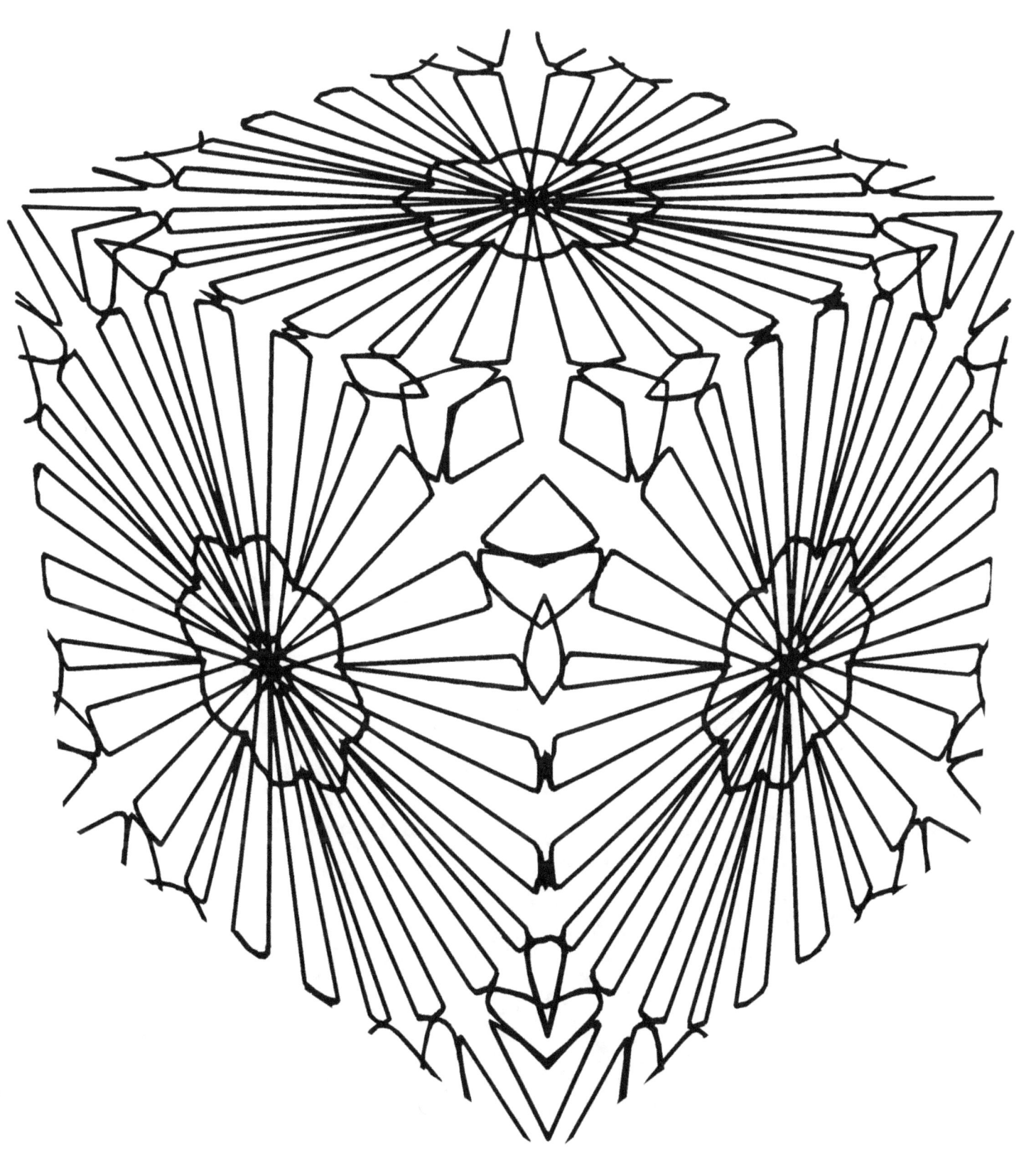

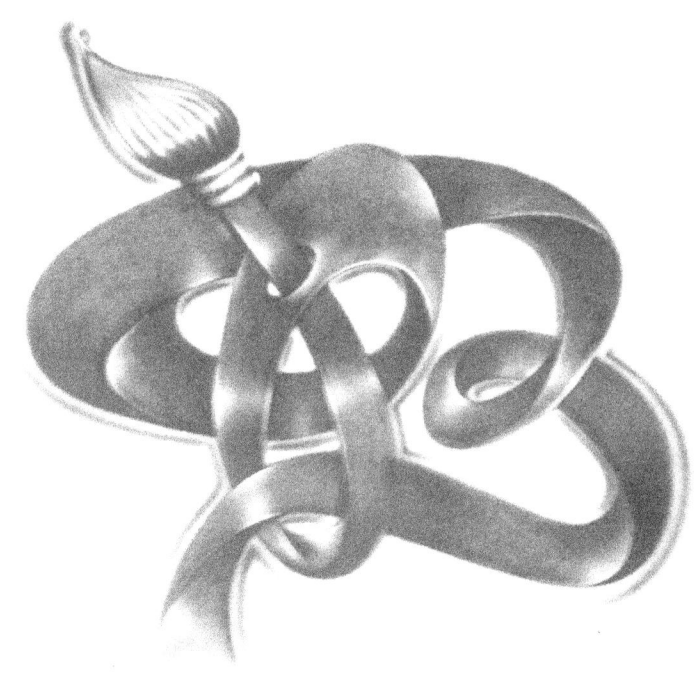

PORTRAITSTHATBREATHE

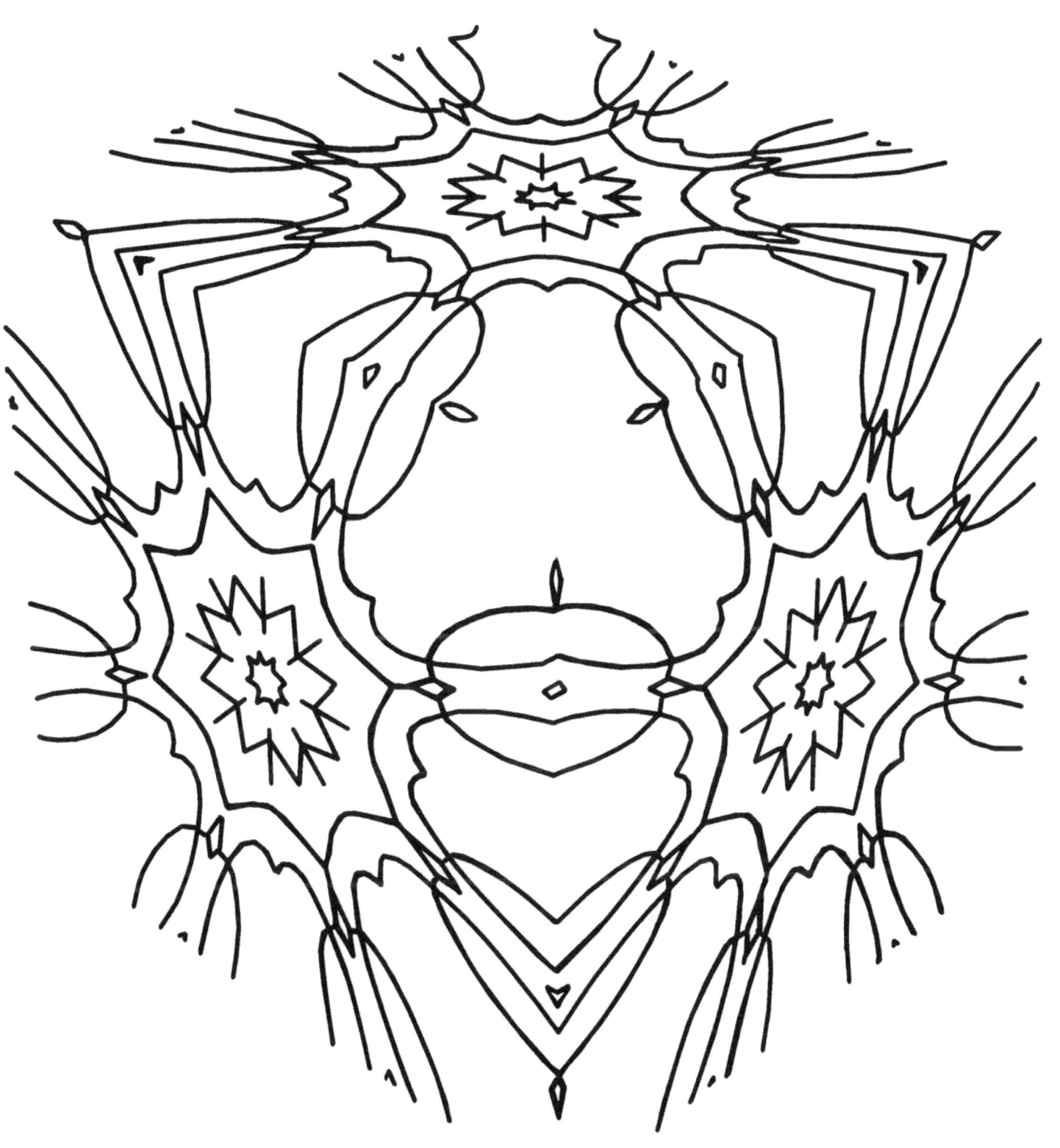

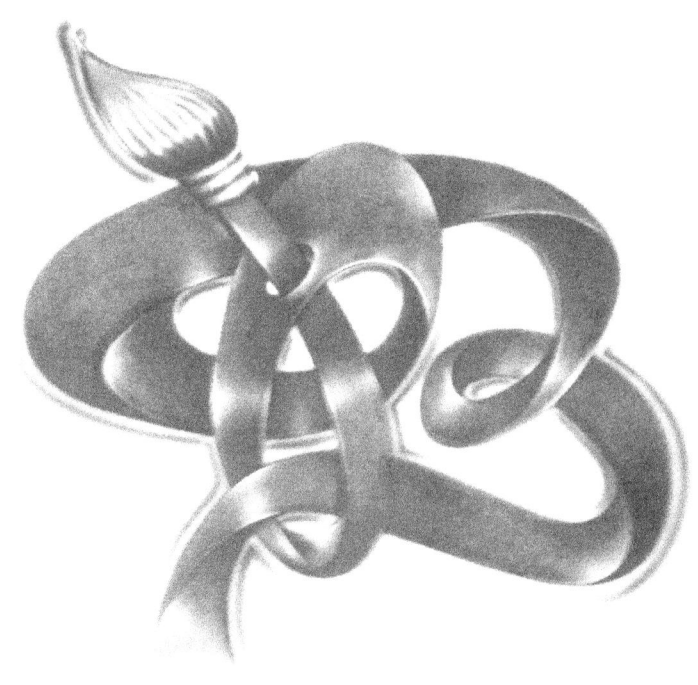

PORTRAITSTHATBREATHE

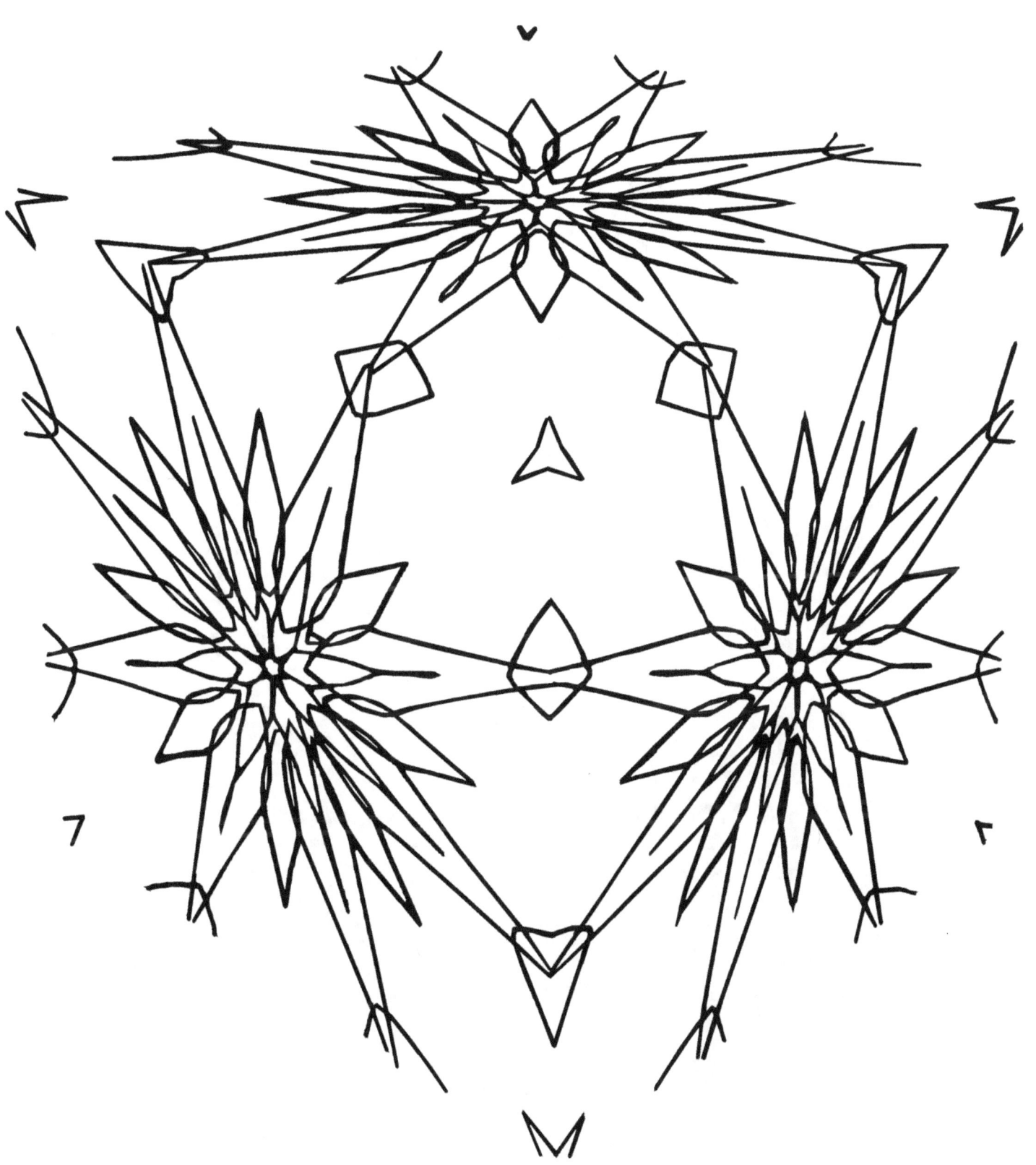

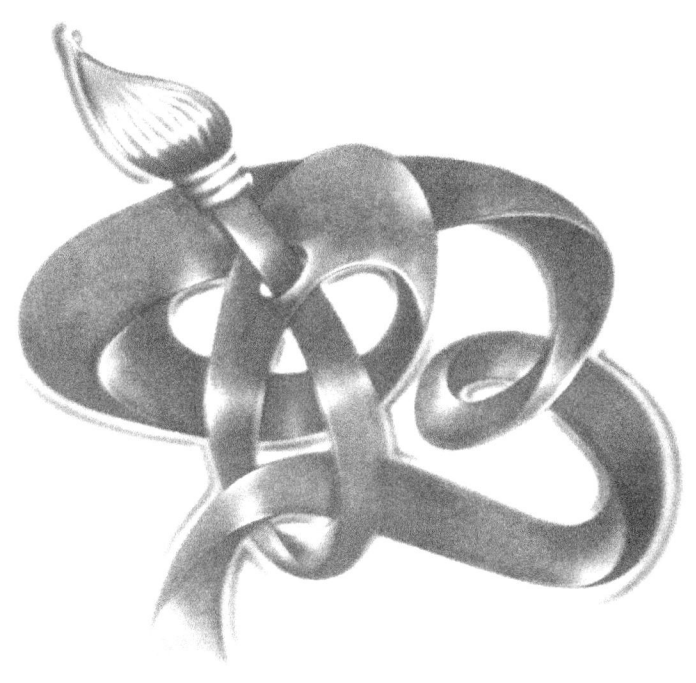

PORTRAITSTHATBREATHE

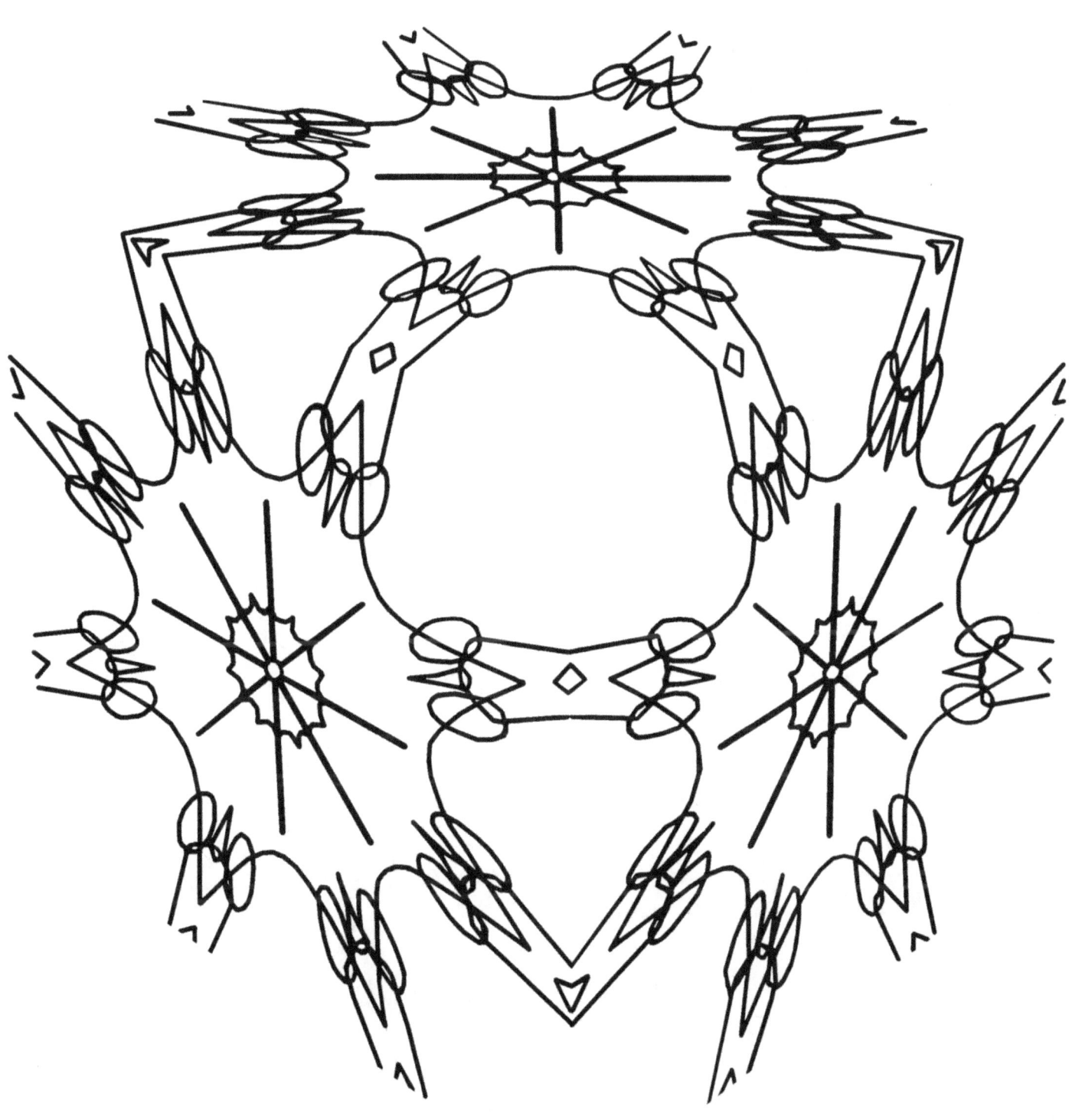

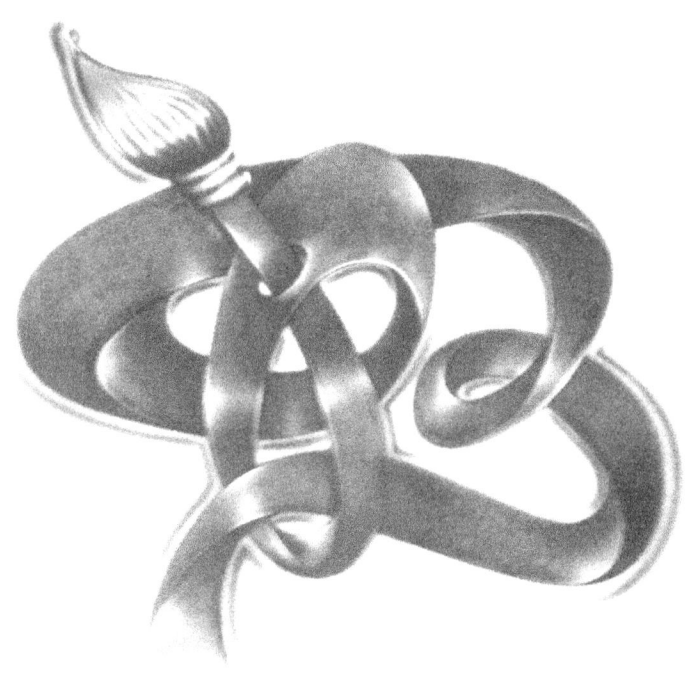

PORTRAITSTHATBREATHE

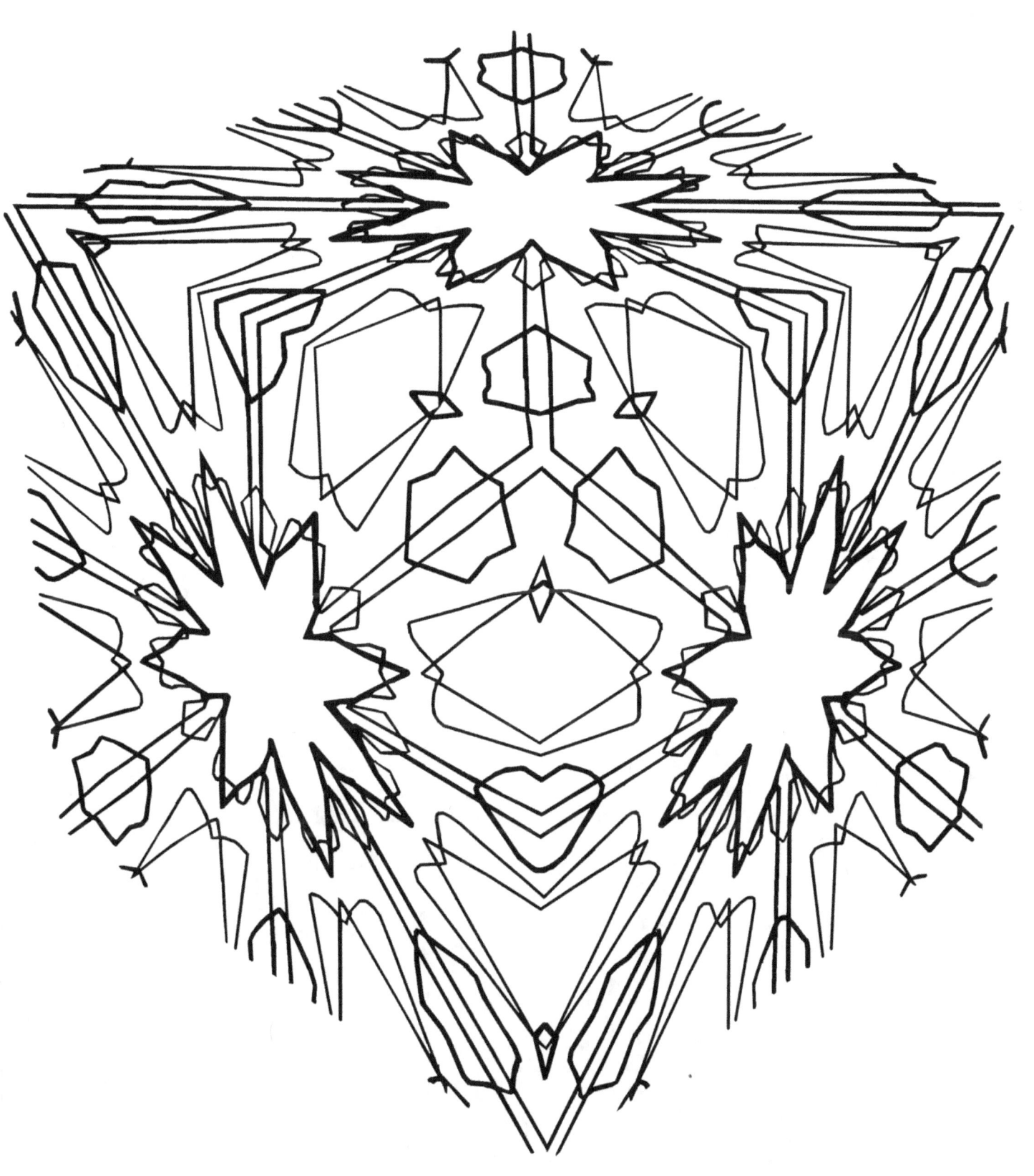

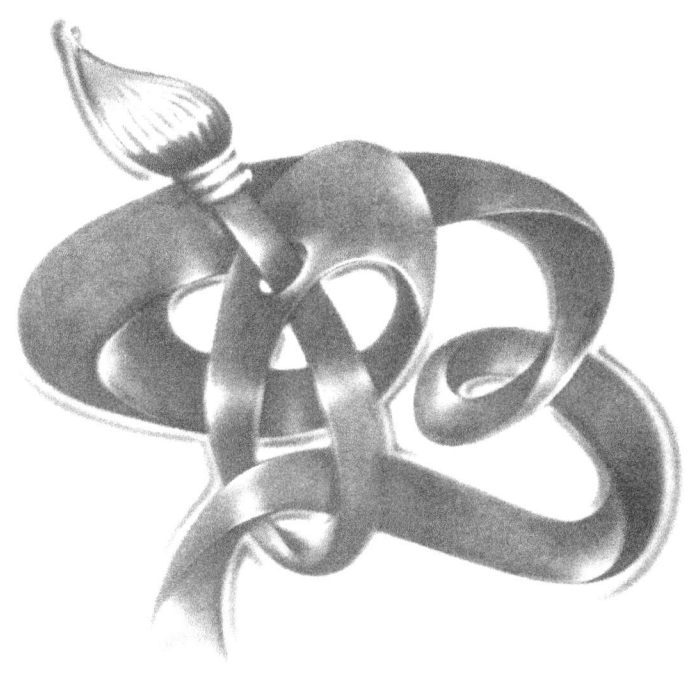

PORTRAITSTHATBREATHE

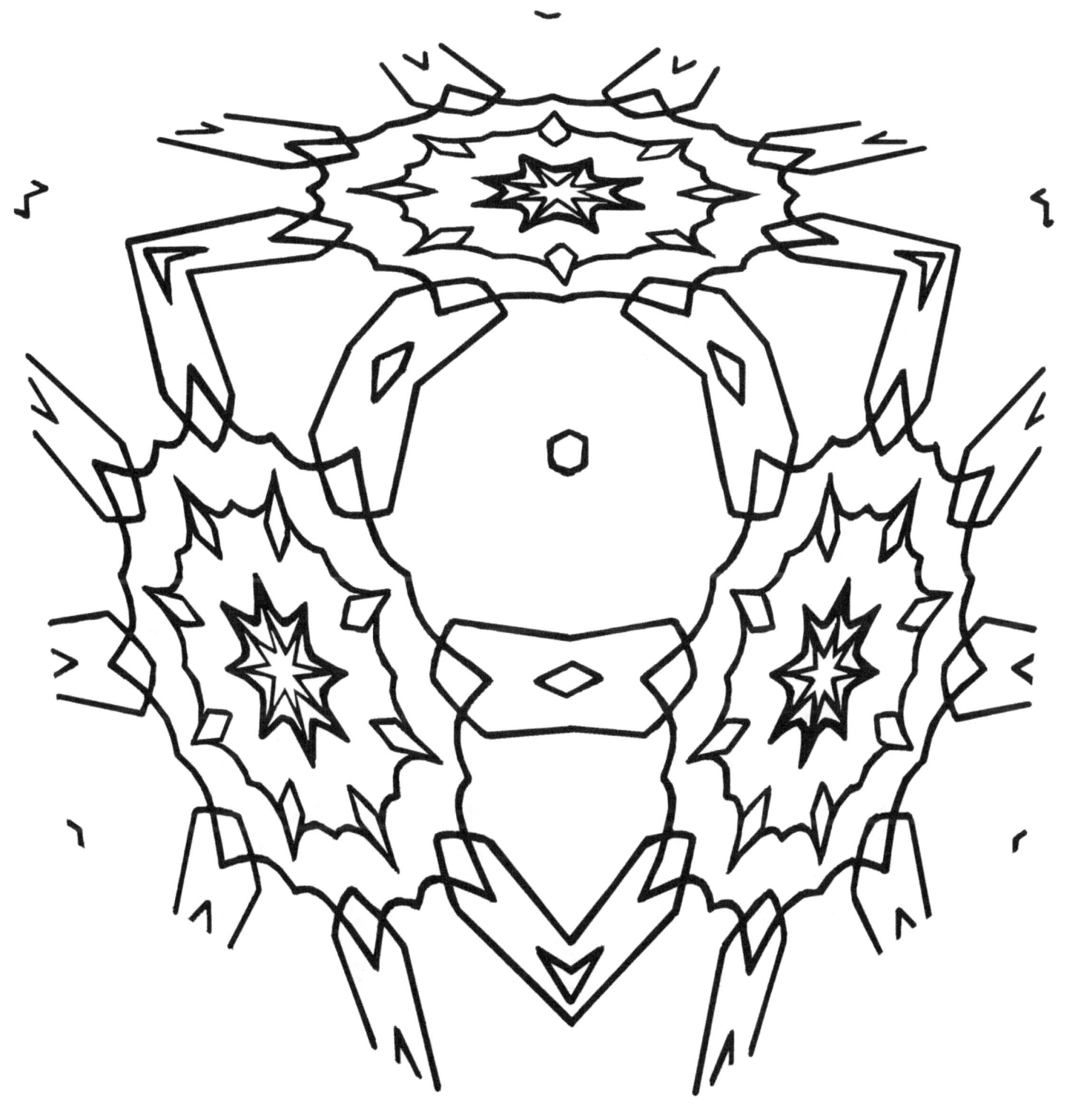

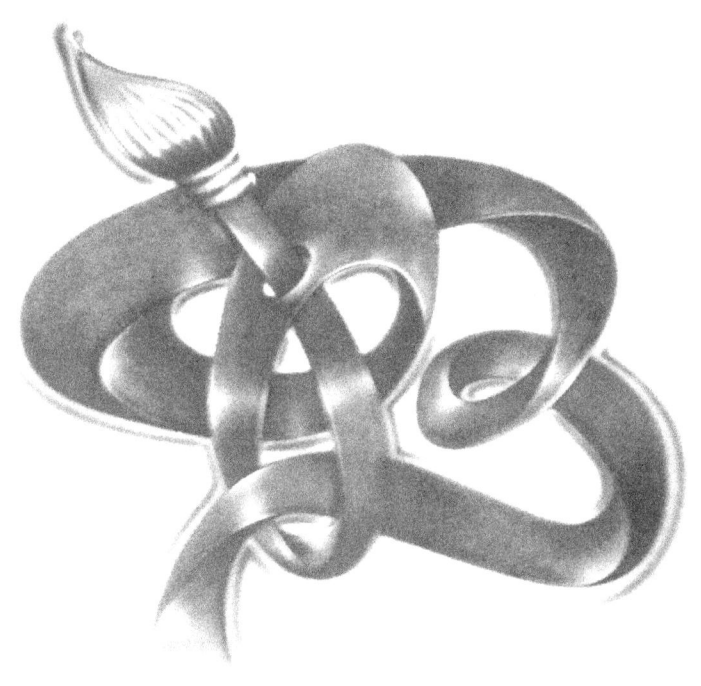

PORTRAITSTHATBREATHE

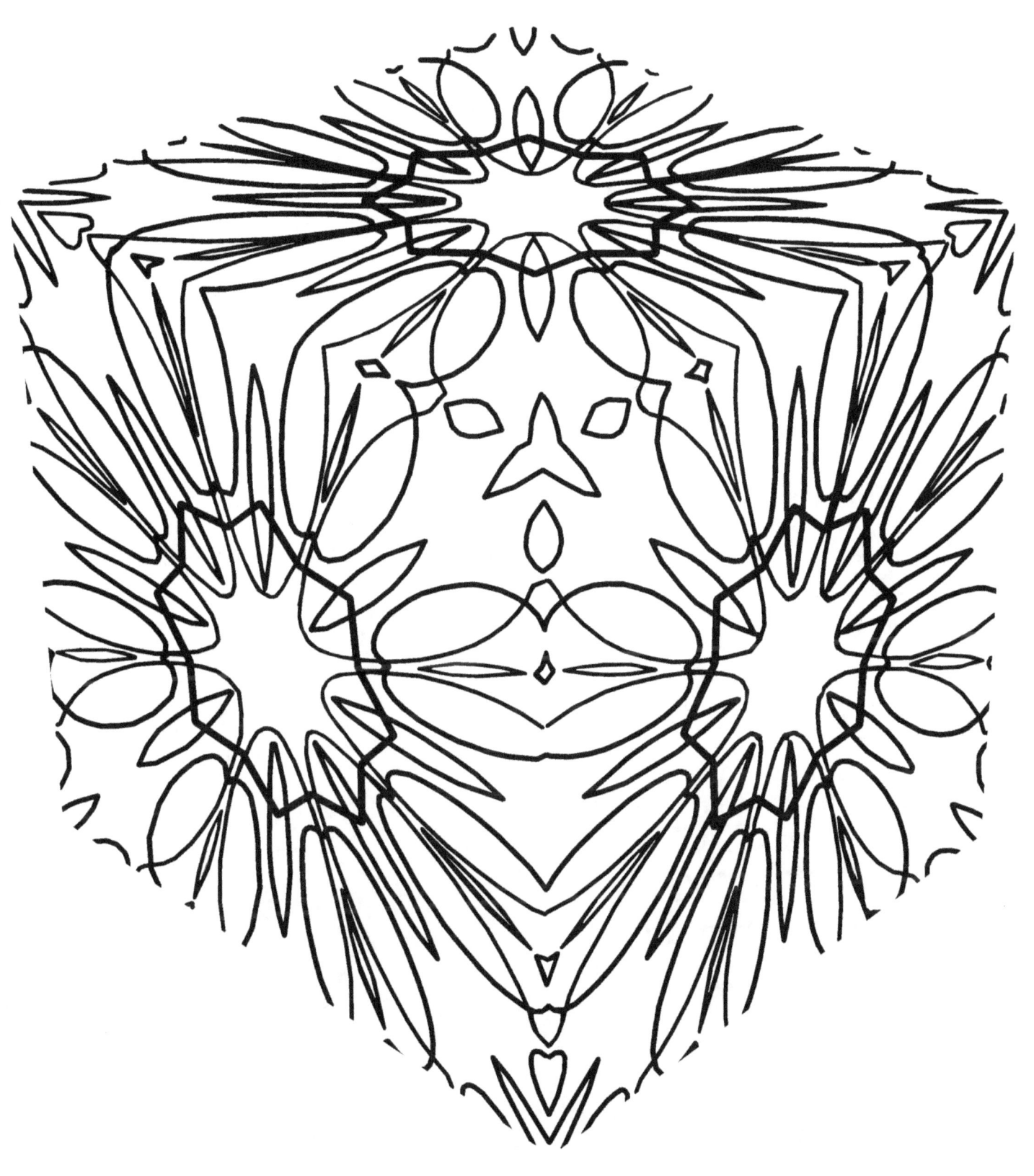

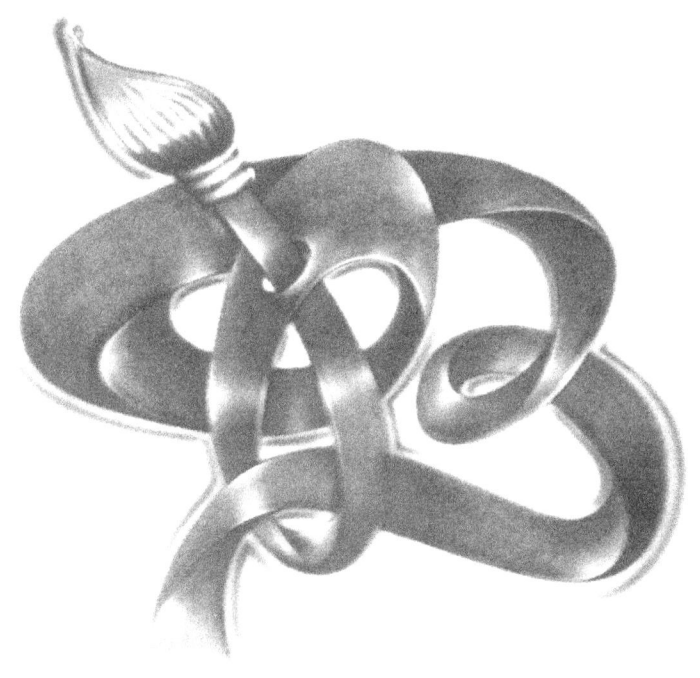

PORTRAITSTHATBREATHE

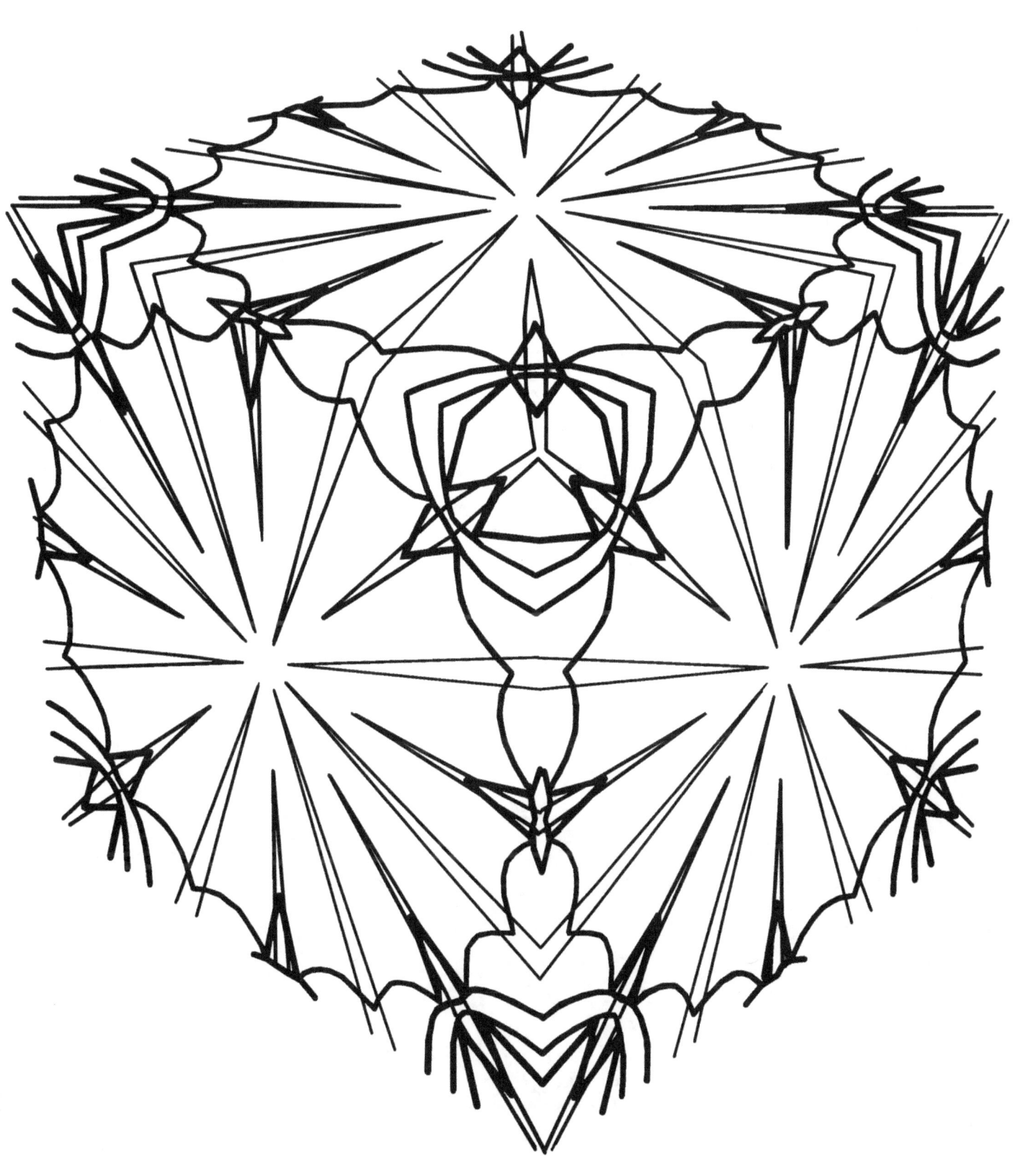

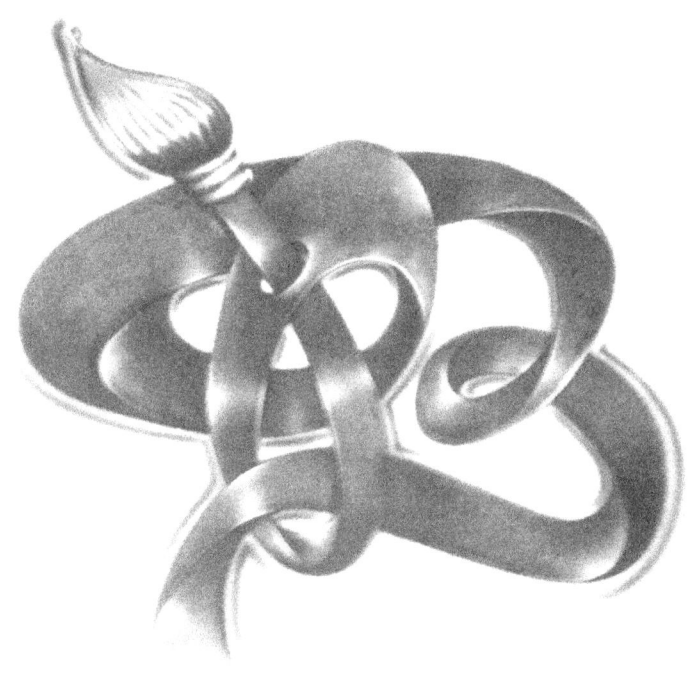

PORTRAITSTHATBREATHE

ACKNOWLEDGMENTS

*I would like to give a special thanks to my wife Tammy of 26 years
For all your loving support.*

*A special acknowledgment to my children: Xavier, Kaman Brielle and Abebe;
In loving memory of my mother Arlean S. Allen; she always gave me Love and
Smile encourage me to do my Best!*

*Special thanks to parent; Charles and Faye Allen; Marvin and Vervela Harris
(Do you like people today?) for your loving support.
Can not forget my brothers; Tony, Gordon, Mike Markel and my sister Zephrea, Jessica Tonya
Michelle and to lil sis in Tennessee. Love to you all always.
A thanks to my uncles and aunts - James, Jimmy and Sunny; Shirley, Barbara, Teen and Ree;
Thank you for believing in me. (remember you bought my very first t-shirts)
Thanks to Howard and Peggy Gibbs for purchasing my very first original canvas painting.
To all my cousin (too many to name) thank you for your love and support - love you all
To my brother in ART! DH2 - Donald Hillsman II, You got the SKILLZ!!!
To my sister Lady Money - Marlese Harris... The Hustle is Real and continues...
To Reggie and Barry from the "D" you (2) helped to take my craft (art) to the next level!!
Donald Hillsman Sr., Thanks for words you once told me "It Is What It Is"
To Gia'na Garel, the Coldest to pick up the pen and paint a Masterpiece with words.
I'm glad "I really know you."
To Barbara G. Middlebrooks, I know what it means to truly have a friend that I can depend
on I really appreciate you helping me get this done, What's Next?*

ABOUT THE AUTHOR

As an artist and entrepreneur of art for almost 35 years, Benjamin Allen takes a specialized, never-before-used process of blending plaster and paint, and creating pieces that offer the soul-stirring 3D effect of coming alive. As a sought after portrait painter, Allen has been commissioned for murals, as a faux finisher, and as a consultant on art related community projects. Acclaimed for his celebrity portraits, Allen has been commissioned by major stars to render their art. In addition to a partnership with Atlanta Designer Sharon Mann, of Sharon Mann Designs, he does faux finishes and painted galaxies across home theater ceilings throughout the region.

Recent clients have included the Tupac Shakur Museum, R&B legend Ronald Isley, The Isley Brothers, Russell Athletics, and murals featured on BRAVO Chnls seasons 1&2 -Married to Medicine; featuring a new Lego superhero mural in Mrs. Toya's son's room.

Allen's art has begun to adorned everything from motorcycles and car tags to bedroom murals, painted marbleized columns and custom painted rooms in show homes, super-sized canvases, and now various sundries and even a clothing/ T-shirt line officially launching in 2017, more at Portraitsthatbreathe.com

www.ingramcontent.com/pod-product-compliance
Lightning Source LLC
Chambersburg PA
CBHW062120220526
45471CB00010B/3816